The Word Made Flesh

Poems By
April Bulmer

ISBN 978-1-55483-577-5 (trpb)

Introduction to
The Word Made Flesh

I recently revisited the stories of Jesus in the
New Testament. I discovered the ancient
texts spoke in the voices of young women
who wished to be heard. I listened. For the
women said: *We are word made flesh...* As a
result, I produced a new rendering of the
classic gospel stories. I hope that my short
narratives are relevant to contemporary
readers and inspire them to lead righteous
lives. I pray they infer that Jesus ministered
to the marginalized and sick. We are called
to address illness and disability too. For the
women of light spoke in tongues: *Darkness
will not overcome.*

1

The shadows of beasts
and the light of
my mother's drooling breasts.
I am born of blood,
tissue and sacrifice.

2

I love the moon
and the star like a jewel
in her turban.
The astrologers bring spices
and kneel before the creche.
They are men of the East
and so tired.
They dream until dusk.

3

John is made of Elizabeth,
Zechariah and the Lord.
John prepares the way
for the Messiah,
opens the loins of River Jordan.

4

I rise from the water.
The Lord descends like a dove.
There is a feather on the wind:
A quill and a drop of blood.

5

Satan blooms red
as a desert flower.
But I dream
he will fade
in the light.

6

Blood and fish
in the womb
of my boat.

7

Follow me,
and I will make
you fishers of all.
But your nets are torn
and your hands are tired
like women who weave
prayer into shawls.

8

Blessed are…
These words nest
in my mouth
and beat like birds
over the mount.

9

A marriage
in Galilee.
Six stone water jars:
Wine for the bridegroom
and his woman.
All that bleed.

10

The sun does not
hide his light
beneath a basket.

11

Woman, you lay sick with fever.
But I take you by the hand,
soon it is cool as stone.
When the sun sets,
I heal more illness
and cast out devils:
Shadows of Capernaum.

12

Lepers of little faith,
be as fowls of the air.
Pray a rosary of seeds.

13

A paralyzed man
births through a hole
in the roof.

14

The Kingdom of God
is like a mustard seed.
All those blooms.
Birds nest in branches
singing to the Lord,
yellow dust on their plumes.

15

She anoints my feet
with ointment and tears.
Dries them with
the pelt of her hair.

16

I cast evil spirits,
infirmities and demons
from the twelve and Mary Magdalene.
They crawl from my disciples
like serpents.

17

Martha's hands move
quickly as doves
while Mary listens
to my parables
and washes my feet.

Blessed is Mary.
I bloom in the womb
of her ear like love.

18

You touch my cloth.
Your faith makes you well.
Only the memory of blood
between the banks
of your bones: A dry river.

19

Take nothing for the journey:
Neither staff nor bag nor bread.
Shake the demons from your feet
as you leave.

20

You will wear my spirit
like gloves:
Your healing hands
soft as newborn doves.

21

I bless a blind man's eyes.
They are black seeds
and bloom in the sun.

22

Crippled woman:
You are crooked and bear a cane.
I lay my hands on your spine.
Your sickness is a serpent.
It slithers away.

23

The corn blooms
on the Sabbath.
The husk opens
like a woman.

24

We cast out spirits
and heal the sick,
though we are sheep
among wolves.
Be wise as serpents,
I tell them,
and innocent as doves.
Spirit will be on your tongue.

25

Do not be afraid, I tell them.
All your hairs are counted.
The long dark strands
rooted like stems.

26

What I say to you
in the dark,
tell in the light.

27

I balance on the sea.
I am not a ghost.
The wind holds its breath.
I leave footsteps on the foam.

28

I am the sun
on a mountain.
I am pale as the Lord
when he birthed the sea.

29

Five thousand awake
with the stink
of fish and barley loaves
on their hands.
They are on their knees.

30

I must go to Jerusalem and suffer
at the hands of the priests,
elders and scribes.
Crucified, but on the third day rise.
I will break from
the womb of a cloud:
Its soft white thighs.

31

You lay your garments
before the colt.
I balance upon the beast.
You sing, *Blessed be.*

32

Mount of Olives
where the dead rest,
dreaming shades of green.

33

The tribes of the earth
bow their heads.
The sun and the moon
close their eyelids.

34

On the day of unleavened bread,
you will reap
wheat and grapes and love.

35

I wash the loose earth
from your feet:
The basin, the water.
You anoint the blue moons
of my knees.

36

I dip the bread
into a bowl
for Judas Iscariot.
It is night.

But in the fullness of time,
the sun will birth his light.

37

In the garden of Gethsemane,
I pray.
My cloth is damp with rain.

38

Peter denies me three times.
A bird opens its hard beak
and mourns.

39

How beautiful the woman
and her alabaster jar.
She anoints my head
with costly ointment.
I will preach the gospel
in memory of her.

40

At Golgotha,
the women wilt
like torn flowers in the dirt:
Faded blossoms
at the base of the cross.

41

People barter for my
clothing and robes.
They tear the warp and weave
of my cloth.
They nail my wrists
to the cross.

42

Why have You forsaken me?
Though nailed to the tree:
I am bark and root and seed.

43

The sun is a purple wound.
The earth quakes.
And the veil
of the temple tears
like a woman.
Graves open:
Bones, the history of milk.

44

Into Your hands
I commend my spirit.
I give up the ghost.

45

Women anoint me with spices.
Wrap me in linen cloth and herbs.
The Lord rolls the stone
from the womb.
The scent of aloe and myrrh.

46

I startle Mary Magdalene
in the garden.
I bloom and fade
and bloom again.
My face is the fabric
of light and rain.

Afterword

Like many forms of artwork, *The Word Made Flesh* is a creative interpretation of the gospel stories. It grew out of the popular belief that the canon welcomes new visions of the narratives. Such a book allows for contemporary talk about Jesus. We require these insights because the words of the Bible are not written in stone. They should be subject to new expressions. For holy text is organic and dynamic. In an open-ended model we are called to add our own voices, homilies and poems to scripture while maintaining some of the main principles of the classic stories. In my case, they are influenced by the concerns of women and new metaphors and images that emerged naturally from my visual sensibility.

Acknowledgments

Photographs included in this book were purchased from 123RF.com. The front-cover photos are called *Figure Hunched Over Under Transparent Cloth* and *Figure Hunched Over Under Cloth*. These shots were taken by rolffimages. The back-cover photo is called *Crucifixion of Good Friday Concept* and was taken by Choat.

Biography

April Bulmer is a Canadian poet. She holds Master's degrees in creative writing, religion and theological studies from major universities. She also earned an Honours B.A. in mass communications and studied dance, music and art history. Much of her writing deals with women and spirituality and the divine feminine. She is also known for her unique imagery. Many of her books have been shortlisted for awards, including the International Beverly Prize for Literature in London, England, the Pat Lowther Memorial Award for the best book of poetry by a Canadian woman, the Next Generation Indie Book Awards in the U.S and the Global Book Awards. She won the YWCA Women of Distinction Award in the art and culture category in Cambridge, Ontario where she lives. April's work has also been celebrated and published widely in prestigious journals, anthologies and newspapers. To contact April Bulmer email april.poet@bell.net.

For further information about April, please see:

www.aprilbulmer.com and
www.aprilbulmer.wordpress.com.